Contents

Some words are shown in bold, **like this**.
You can find them in the glossary on page 23.

What is an aeroplane?

aeroplane

An aeroplane is a **vehicle** that flies through the sky.

Some planes are big enough to carry hundreds of passengers a long way.

runway

You get on an aeroplane at a place called an airport.

At the airport, planes take off and land down a long track called a runway.

Why might I go on an aeroplane?

You might have friends or family who live a long way away.

Travelling by aeroplane can be the quickest way to visit them.

You might travel by aeroplane when you go on holiday.

An aeroplane can take you to new, exciting places.

What should I take for my trip?

suitcase

Pack a suitcase with everything you will need while you are away.

During the flight, your suitcase will be stored in the plane's **hold**.

hand-luggage

You should also pack a small bag with quiet things to do during your journey.

You could take a story, a sticker book, and a colouring pad and crayons.

What will happen at the airport?

At the airport, first you **check in** your suitcases.

Airport staff label the suitcases and send them to be stored in the **hold** of your plane.

Other airport workers will check your aeroplane ticket and **passport**.

There is special equipment to check that nothing you are carrying breaks safety rules.

What happens when I get on the plane?

You may have to wait a while before your plane is ready for you to get on.

Then you walk down a long corridor called a jetway to the aeroplane door.

The space where everyone sits is called the **cabin**.

One of the **cabin crew** will help you find your seat and put away your bag.

Does the aeroplane take off straight away?

Before the plane can take off, there are lots of safety checks to be done.

Everyone must wear their seat belts and listen to safety instructions from the crew.

When the aeroplane is ready to take off, the **engines** make a lot of noise.

The plane speeds faster and faster along the runway, then tilts up into the air!

What happens when the aeroplane is in the sky?

When the plane is high in the sky, you may be allowed to undo your seat belt.

On some flights, you may get to watch TV or have a meal.

You might want to read a book or play with the colouring set you brought with you in your hand luggage.

You can also use the toilet.

What happens when the aeroplane lands?

When the aeroplane is ready to land, you must put on your seat belt.

Your ears might feel funny as the aeroplane gets closer to the ground.

When the plane's wheels touch down on the runway, it can be a bit bumpy.

The plane makes a lot of noise as it slows down and stops.

What do I do after the aeroplane lands?

suitcase

When the aeroplane stops, you can take off your seat belt, pick up your bag, and walk into the airport.

Then it's time to collect your suitcase.

You might pass through some more security checks, then you can leave the airport.

Your exciting aeroplane trip is over.

List of hand luggage items

Do pack:

- ✓ a favourite soft toy
- ✓ a book or comic
- ✓ a quiet game to play
- ✓ a colouring set
- ✓ a piece of fruit or a snack.

Don't pack:

- ✗ any liquids, such as toys filled with water
- ✗ a drink (you can buy a drink when you have gone through the airport security checks)
- ✗ anything sharp, such as scissors
- ✗ anything that could make a mess if it spills or melts
- ✗ anything that breaks easily.

Picture glossary

 **cabin** place inside an aeroplane where people sit

 **cabin crew** people who work on an aeroplane. They look after you on your journey and make sure you are safe.

 **check in** hand your suitcases over to airport staff so they can put them in the aeroplane

 **engine** machine that powers another machine, to make it go

 **hold** part of an aeroplane that is used to store suitcases

 **passport** special type of small book that contains information about you, such as your name and date of birth

 **vehicle** any type of transport that can carry people or things from place to place

Find out more

Books

First Plane Trip (Fred Bear and Friends), Melanie Joyce (TickTock Books, 2007)

Going on a Plane (First Experiences), Anna Civardi (Usborne, 2005)

What Happens at an Airport? (Where People Work), Amy Hutchings (Weekly Reader Early Learning Library, 2009)

Websites

Learn more about how aeroplanes and airports work at:
www.boeing.com/companyoffices/aboutus/kids/

Find out how aeroplanes get up into the air at:
www.boeing.com/companyoffices/aboutus/wonder_of_flight/index.html

Index